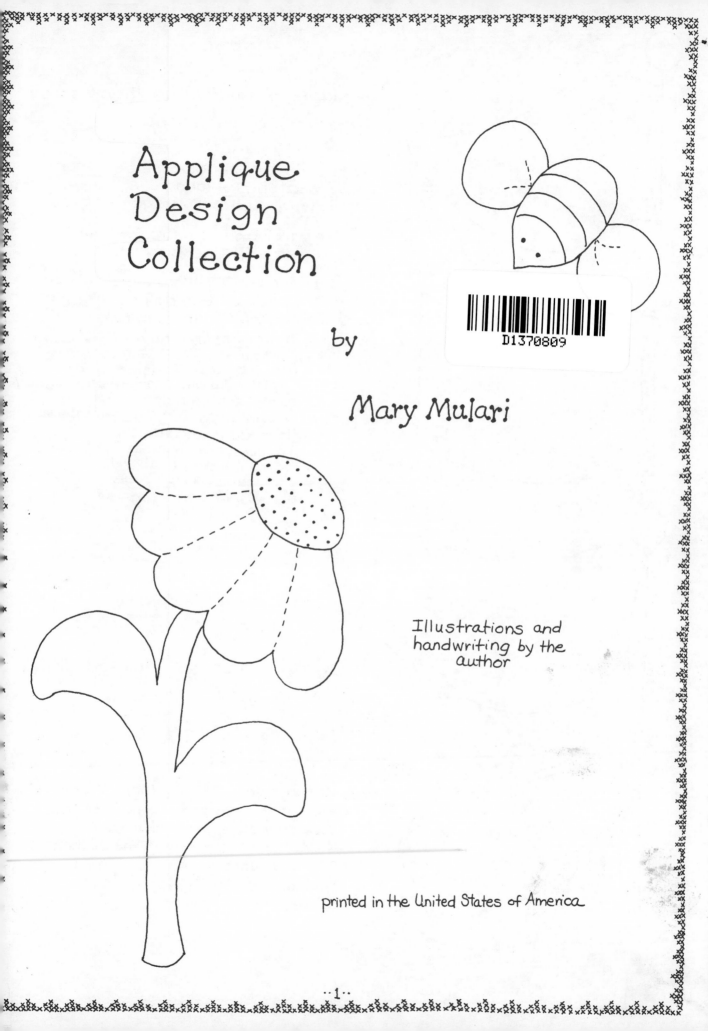

Applique Design Collection

by

Mary Mulari

Illustrations and
handwriting by the
author

printed in the United States of America

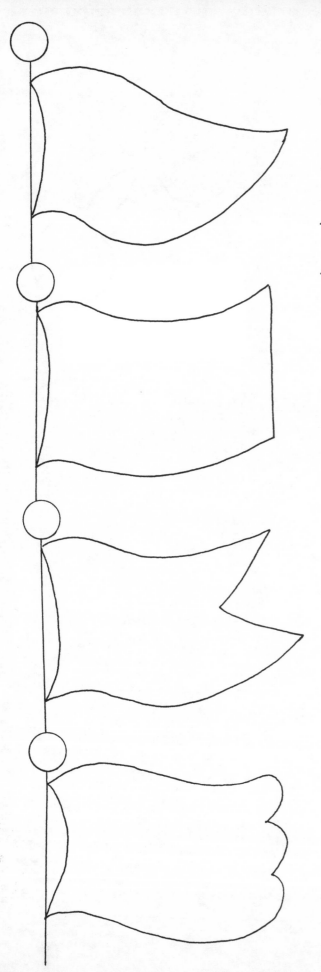

Flags to salute and thank these very special people:

~ Friends and readers of <u>Designer Sweatshirts</u> who have offered ideas and encouragement

~ Margaret and Dan Croswell who helped with the birds

~ Family members who joined me for a modeling session on the shores of Pot Lake in Palo:

    Helmi Koski - my mother
      "mom" design - page 27
    Mary B. Koski - sister-in-law
      pink tulip with heart flowers - page 24
    Sarah Koski - niece
      paintbrush with rainbow - page 46
    John Koski - nephew
      "Hooked on Minnesota" - page 33
    Barry Mulari - husband
      Canada Goose - page 4
My ❤ design - page 28

ISBN 0-9613569-3-6

Seventh Printing - March 1988

Table of Contents

Lily of the Valley

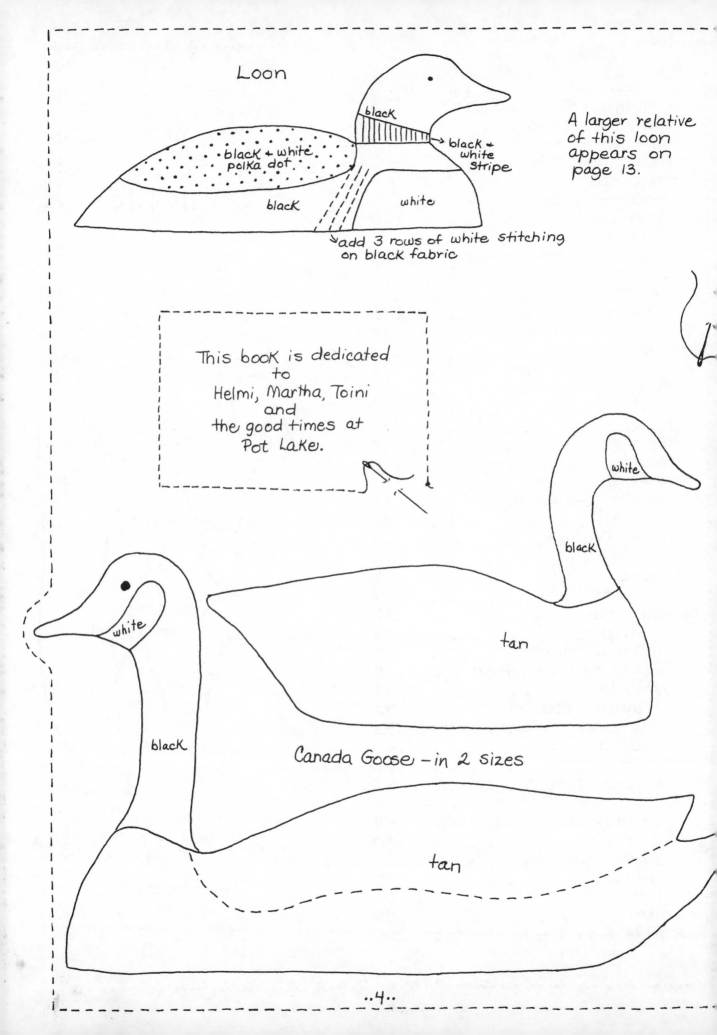

Loon

black

black + white
polka dot

black → black + white stripe

black

white

add 3 rows of white stitching on black fabric

A larger relative of this loon appears on page 13.

This book is dedicated
to
Helmi, Martha, Toini
and
the good times at
Pot Lake.

white

black

tan

white

black

Canada Goose – in 2 sizes

tan

Introduction
(or How this Book Came About...)

As I developed a sweatshirt decorating class and wrote my first book, Designer Sweatshirts, I realized the need for a selection of applique patterns. I have been encouraged by readers and students to develop this collection. I have attempted to create a variety of designs and hope your favorite shapes and motifs are represented. Please use your own imagination and ideas to alter or embellish my designs. I will be glad if they inspire you.

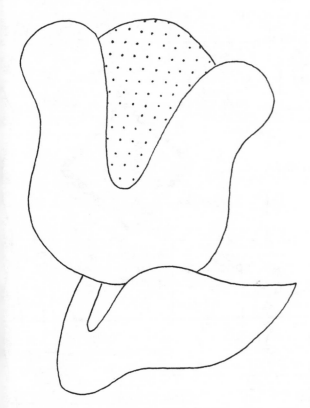

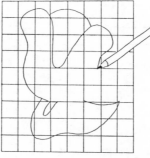

To enlarge or reduce a design from this book:

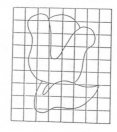

Trace the design from the book. Mark the tracing with lines to form squares of ½".

Mark another piece of paper with the same number of squares in a larger size (to enlarge) or a smaller size (to reduce). Copy each square of the design from your original traced design to the second set of squares you drew.

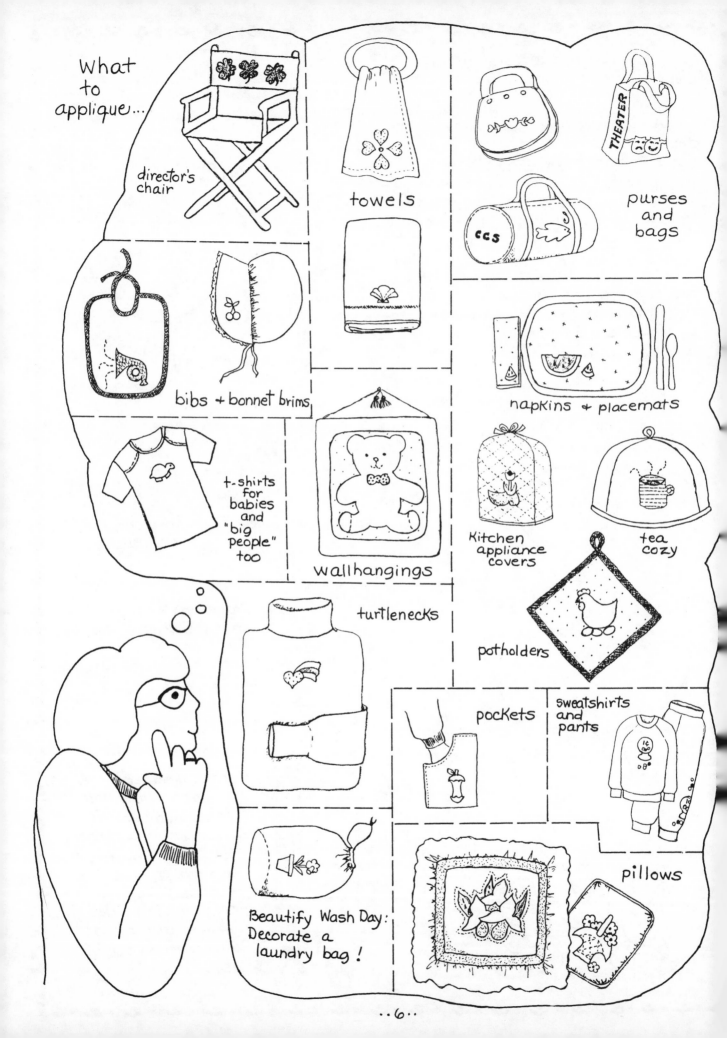

What to applique...

director's chair

towels

purses and bags

CCS

THEATER

bibs + bonnet brims

napkins + placemats

kitchen appliance covers

tea cozy

t-shirts for babies and "big people" too

wallhangings

potholders

turtlenecks

pockets

sweatshirts and pants

Beautify Wash Day: Decorate a laundry bag!

pillows

Applique Hints

To achieve a professional look in machine applique stitching, you will need to practice and to become familiar with the capabilities of your sewing machine. Here are a few hints to make the stitching easier and consistent, particularly on knit fabrics:

1. Use good quality thread and a new needle.

2. To add stability to cotton fabrics you select for applique shapes, you may want to use lightweight fusible interfacing. Cut a piece of fabric a little larger than the applique design, fuse interfacing to the back of the fabric, and cut out the design. The edges of the applique will be more stable and will not fray easily.

3. Loosen the top tension on your sewing machine. This brings the top thread to the bottom side of the fabric and creates smooth topstitching.

4. Attach applique pieces firmly to the fabric onto which they will be sewn. Use Stitch Witchery, gluestick, or many short (sequin) pins.

5. Pin a piece of tear-away pellon or typing paper under the design area on the back of the fabric. This will help your machine feed dogs to operate more evenly as you stitch and will prevent a "wavy" surface on the stitching. Remove and discard the paper or pellon after you finish stitching.

More complete instructions for applique can be found in my first book, Designer Sweatshirts.

How to Use This Book and the Patterns

As you turn the pages of this book, you will notice that it has been organized by categories. There is also an index to help you locate specific designs.

You will notice dashed lines (------) as part of many of the designs. These lines indicate stitching lines which can be added by machine or by hand embroidery in matching or contrasting thread color. For example, the onion roots on the design on this page can be added with applique stitching with brown thread.

When you select a design to use, trace it from the book onto a piece of tracing or typing paper. Cut the design out of the paper, cutting it into pieces if it has several parts. If you want to reverse the design to face in the opposite direction, flip the design pieces over.

Next you will cut the design from fabric, remembering to add an extension to any pieces that will overlap. You would cut the green onion stem about 1/4" longer, as indicated by the dotted line on the design, so it could be slipped under the white section.

To transfer the dashed lines to the fabric, you can use dressmaker's tracing paper or use your own judgement and draw freehand with a washable marking pen.

For small details such as eyes on faces, you could use the machine applique stitch to fill in a small area. Small buttons can also be used. If you like to do machine embroidery, fill in details or larger areas of the design with machine stitching. Also consider hand embroidery.

To prepare the designs for hand-stitched applique, add a seam allowance (about 1/4") around each edge of the design. This will be turned under as you stitch.

To save design pieces and to store other applique patterns, you might like to tape or glue an envelope inside the cover of this book.

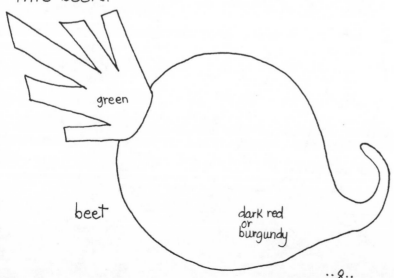

beet — dark red or burgundy — green

And now the designs...

A is for Apple.

← Cut this apple shape from red fabric to represent a whole apple. Cut from white fabric and stitch with red thread to represent half an apple.

← stitching lines for half an apple

apple slice

red

← brown stem

red

this worm can peek from the side of this apple

white

red

an "apple-qued" apron for an orchard owner teacher apple-lover anyone

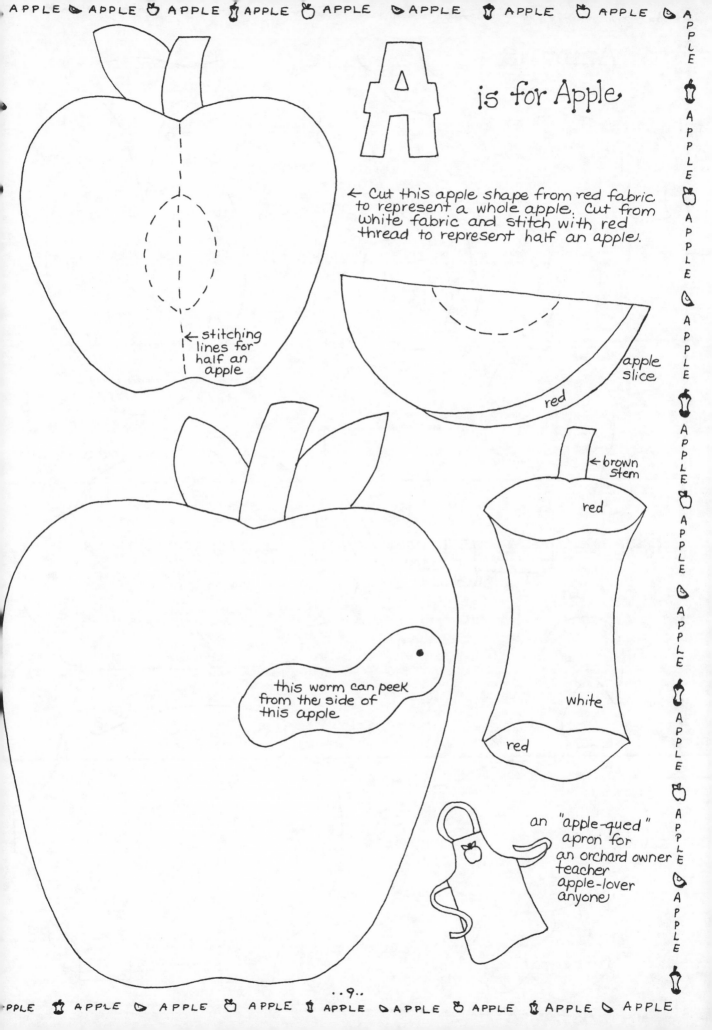

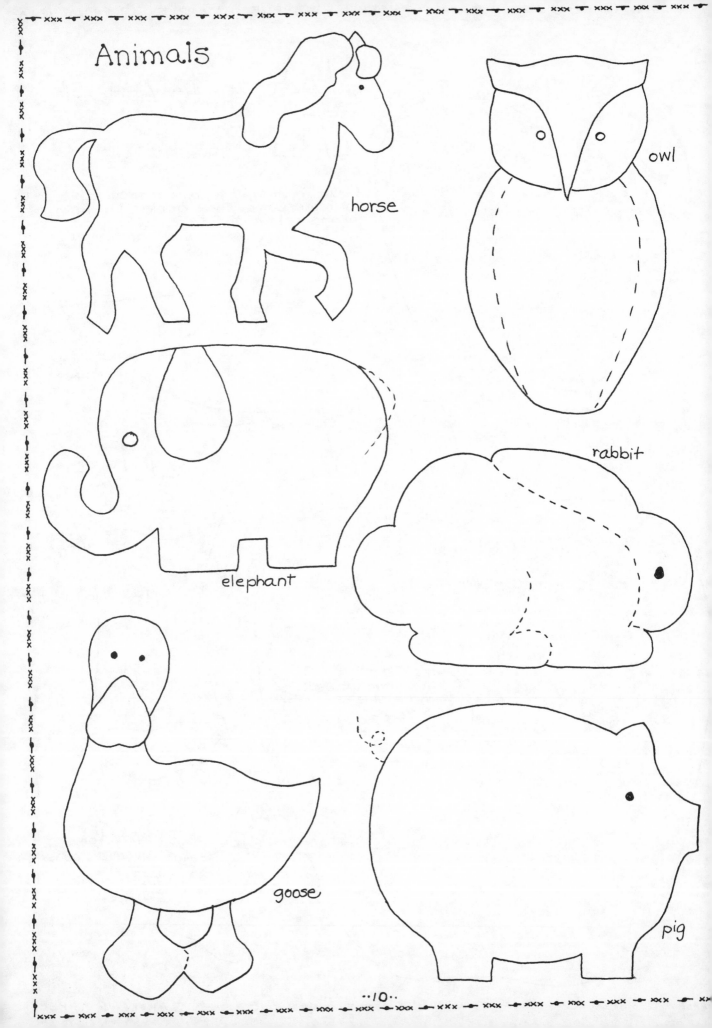

Animals

horse

owl

elephant

rabbit

goose

pig

Animals

black or white sheep

use fake fur (sheepskin) for the body to get an authentic look.

giraffe

use white fabric or white fake fur for this part of the penguin

penguin

moose

Cats 'n Dogs

Add a narrow ribbon or
a bow around the neck
for special trim.

poodle

A Loon and Other Birds

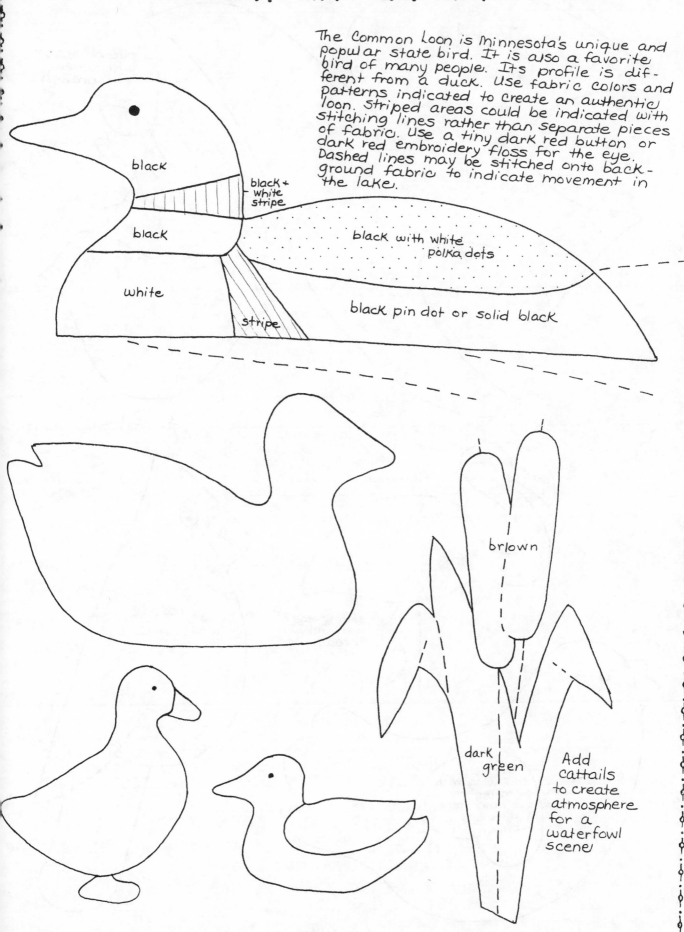

The Common Loon is Minnesota's unique and popular state bird. It is also a favorite bird of many people. Its profile is different from a duck. Use fabric colors and patterns indicated to create an authentic loon. Striped areas could be indicated with stitching lines rather than separate pieces of fabric. Use a tiny dark red button or dark red embroidery floss for the eye. Dashed lines may be stitched onto background fabric to indicate movement in the lake.

black

black + white stripe

black

white

stripe

black with white polka dots

black pin dot or solid black

brown

dark green

Add cattails to create atmosphere for a waterfowl scene

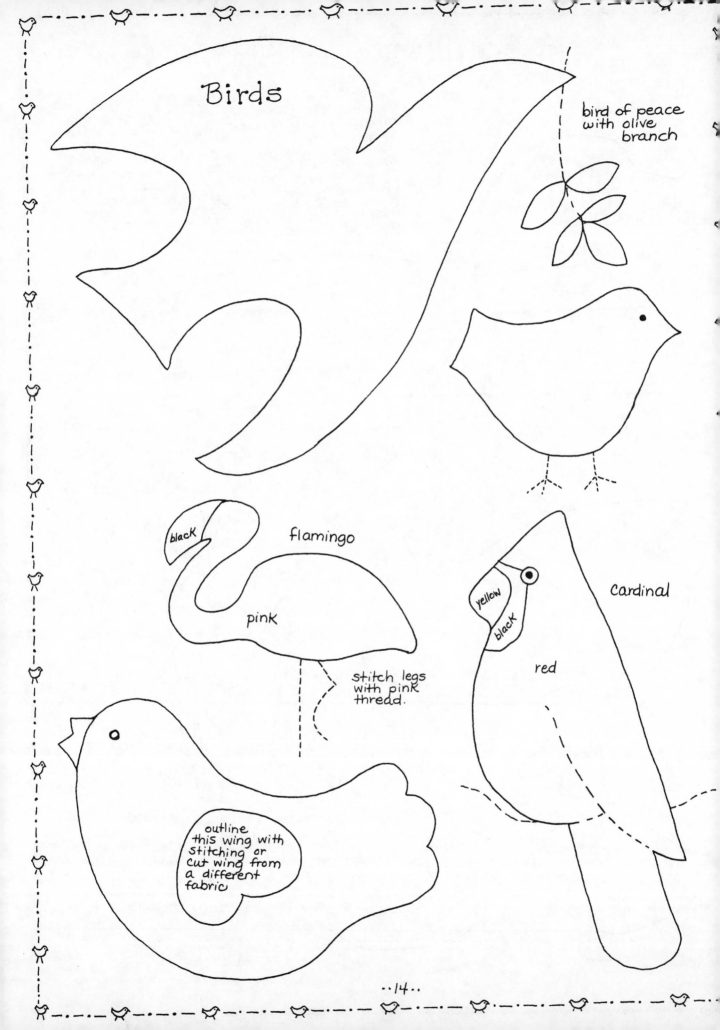

Birds

bird of peace
with olive
branch

black

flamingo

pink

stitch legs
with pink
thread.

cardinal

yellow

black

red

outline
this wing with
stitching or
cut wing from
a different
fabric

Christmas

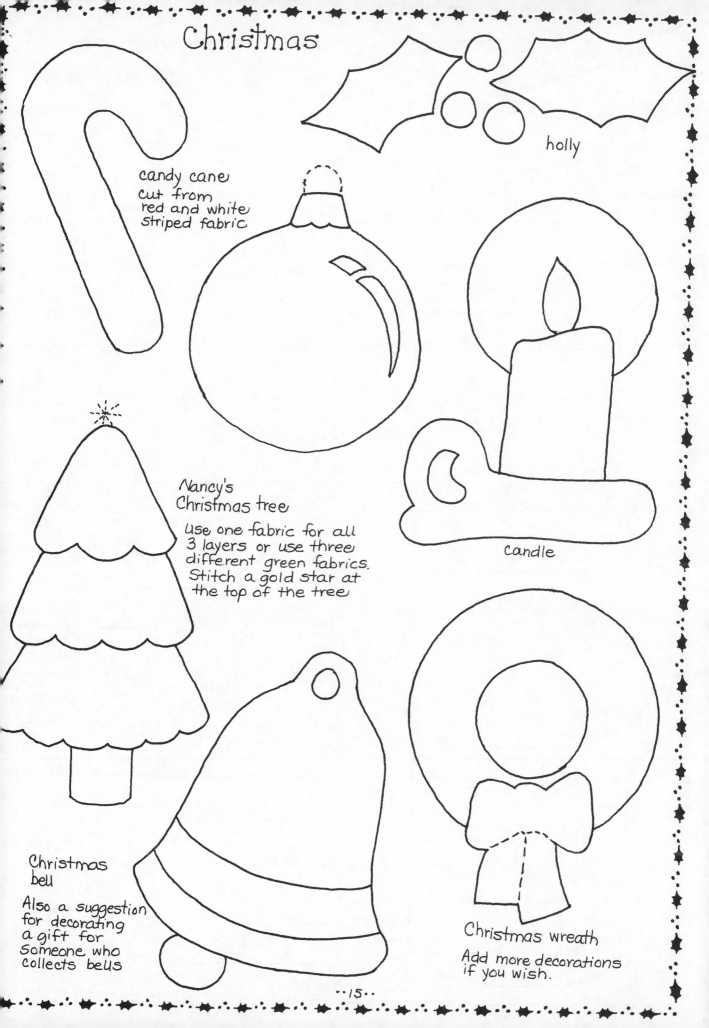

holly

candy cane
cut from
red and white
striped fabric

candle

Nancy's
Christmas tree

Use one fabric for all
3 layers or use three
different green fabrics.
Stitch a gold star at
the top of the tree

Christmas
bell

Also a suggestion
for decorating
a gift for
someone who
collects bells

Christmas wreath

Add more decorations
if you wish.

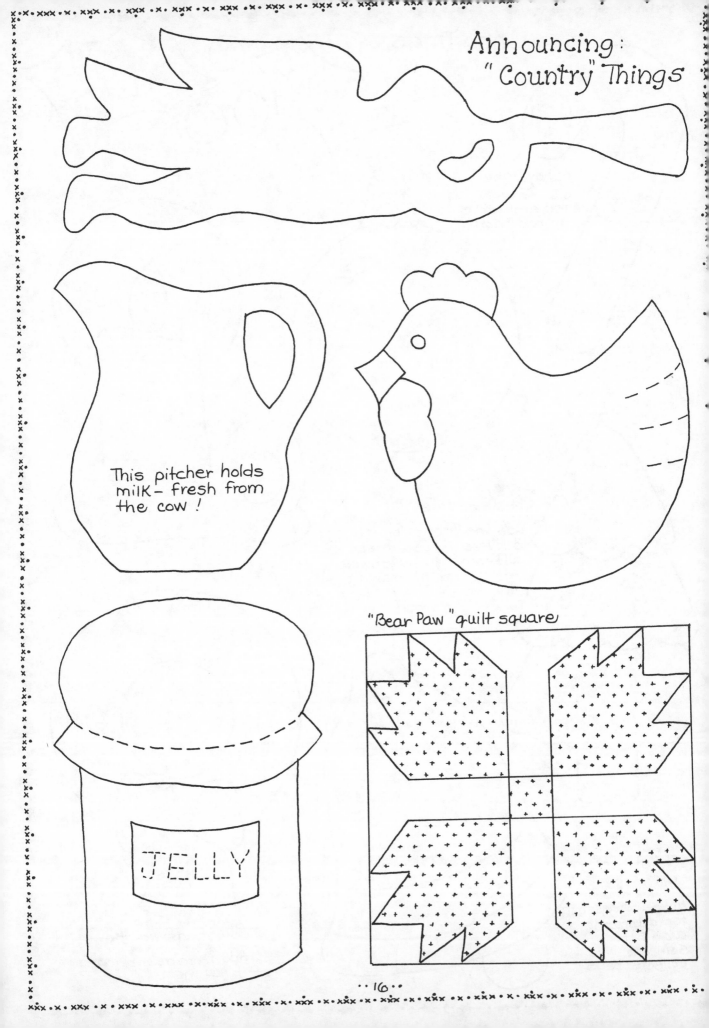

This pitcher holds milk- fresh from the cow!

JELLY

"Bear Paw" quilt square

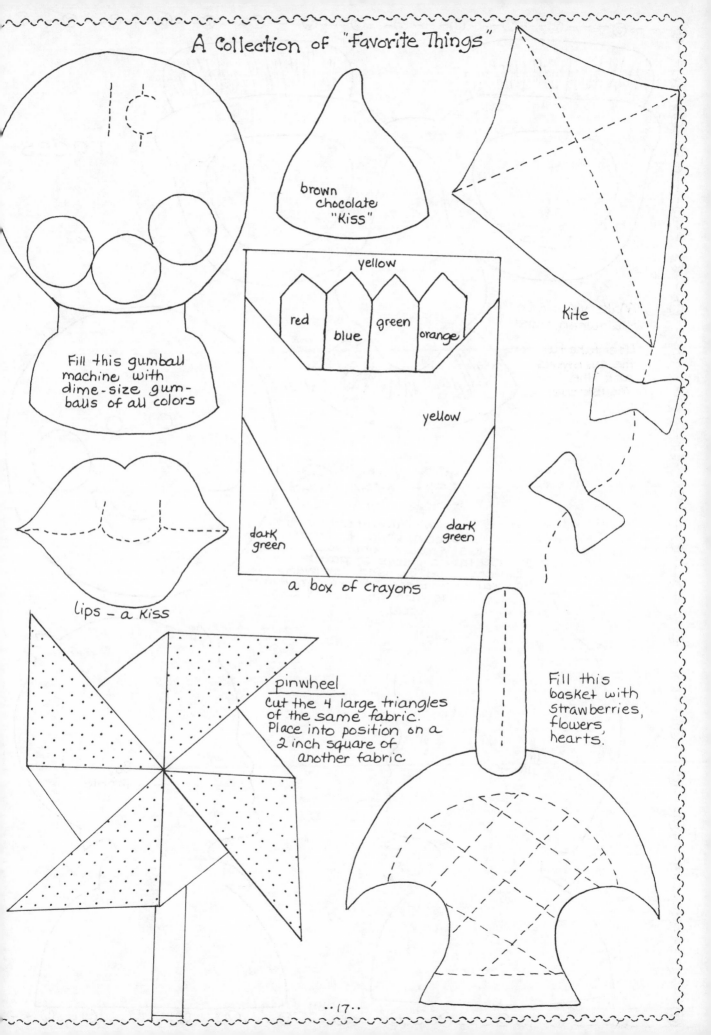

1¢

brown chocolate "Kiss"

Kite

Fill this gumball machine with dime-size gumballs of all colors

yellow

red
blue
green
orange

yellow

dark green

dark green

a box of crayons

lips – a Kiss

pinwheel
Cut the 4 large triangles of the same fabric. Place into position on a 2 inch square of another fabric

Fill this basket with strawberries, flowers, hearts.

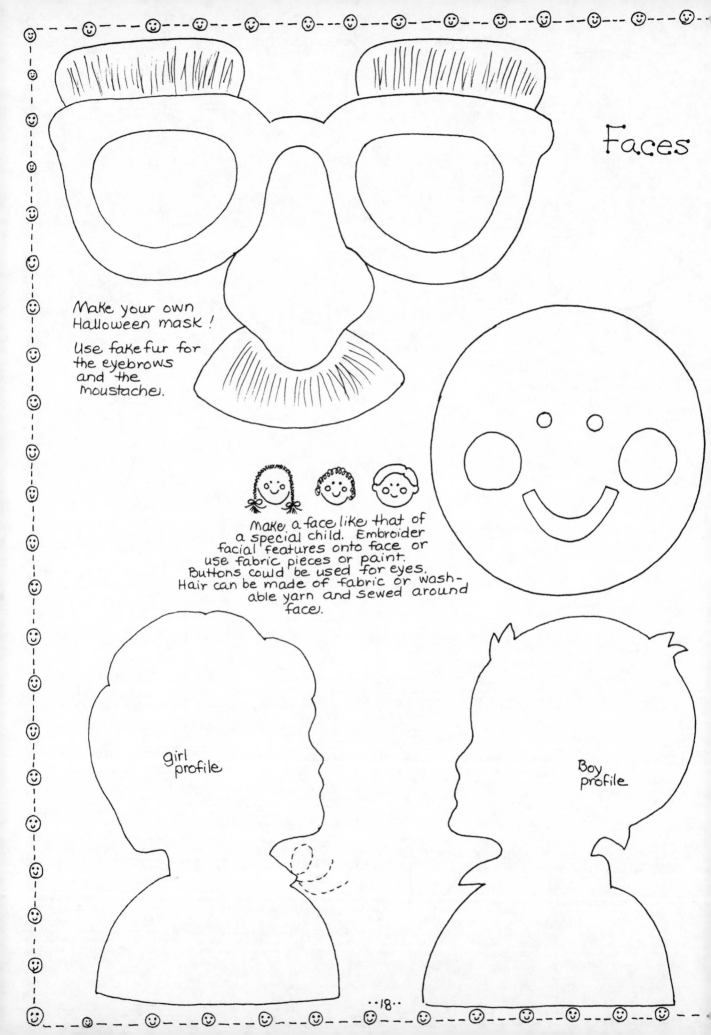

Faces

Make your own Halloween mask!

Use fake fur for the eyebrows and the moustache.

Make a face like that of a special child. Embroider facial features onto face or use fabric pieces or paint. Buttons could be used for eyes. Hair can be made of fabric or wash-able yarn and sewed around face.

girl profile

Boy profile

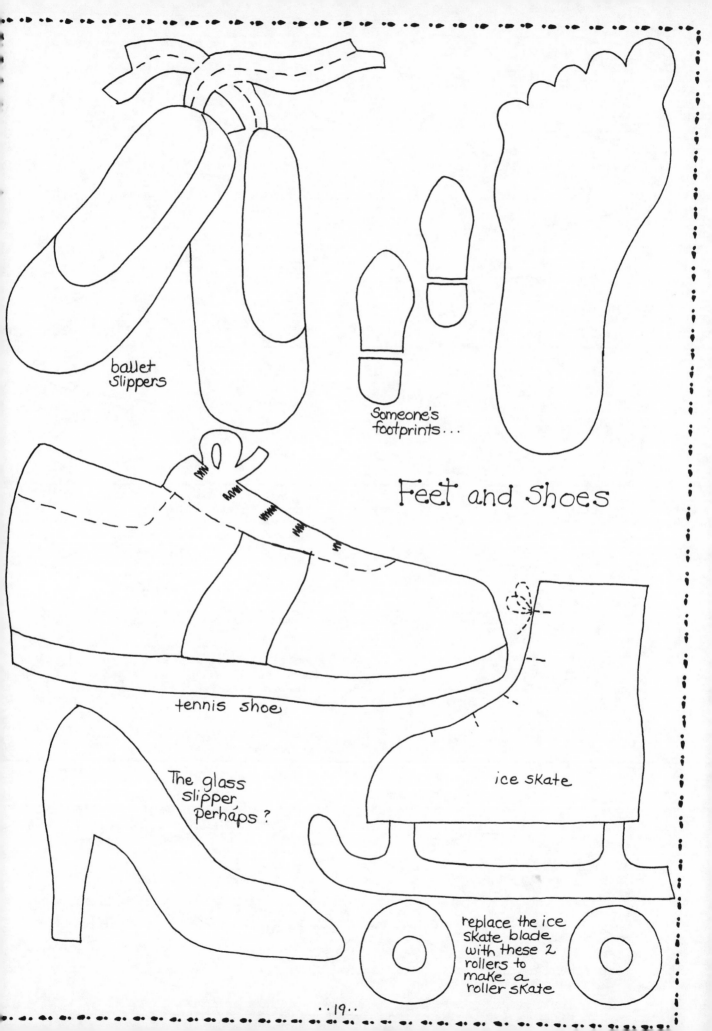

ballet
slippers

Someone's
footprints...

Feet and Shoes

tennis shoe

ice skate

The glass
slipper
perhaps?

replace the ice
skate blade
with these 2
rollers to
make a
roller skate

Fish

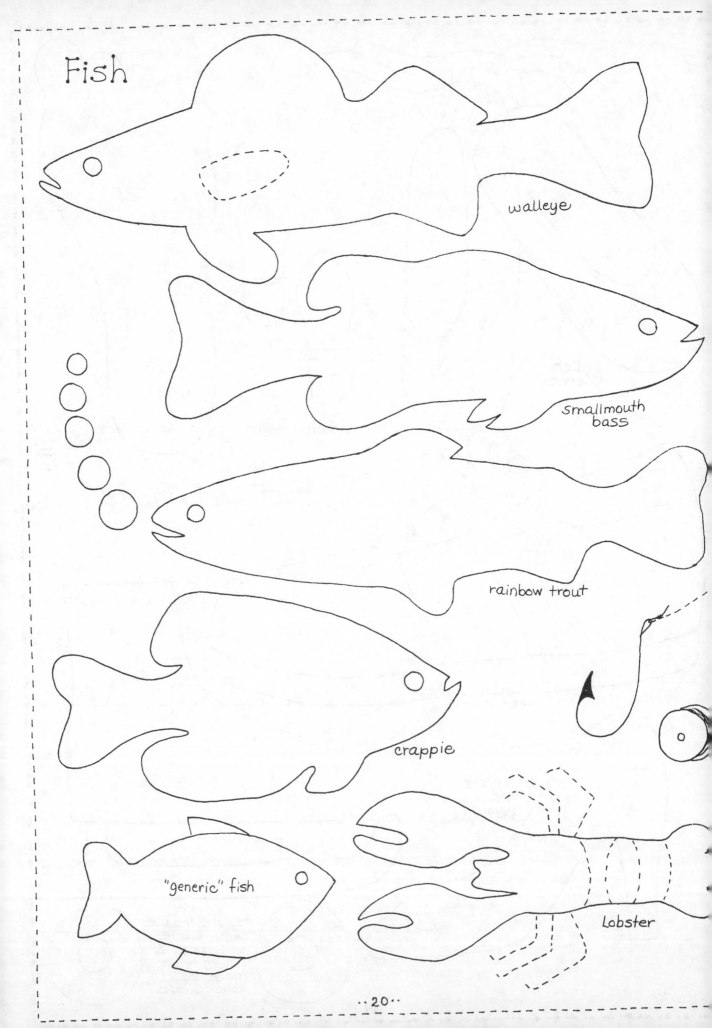

walleye

smallmouth bass

rainbow trout

crappie

"generic" fish

Lobster

Fruit

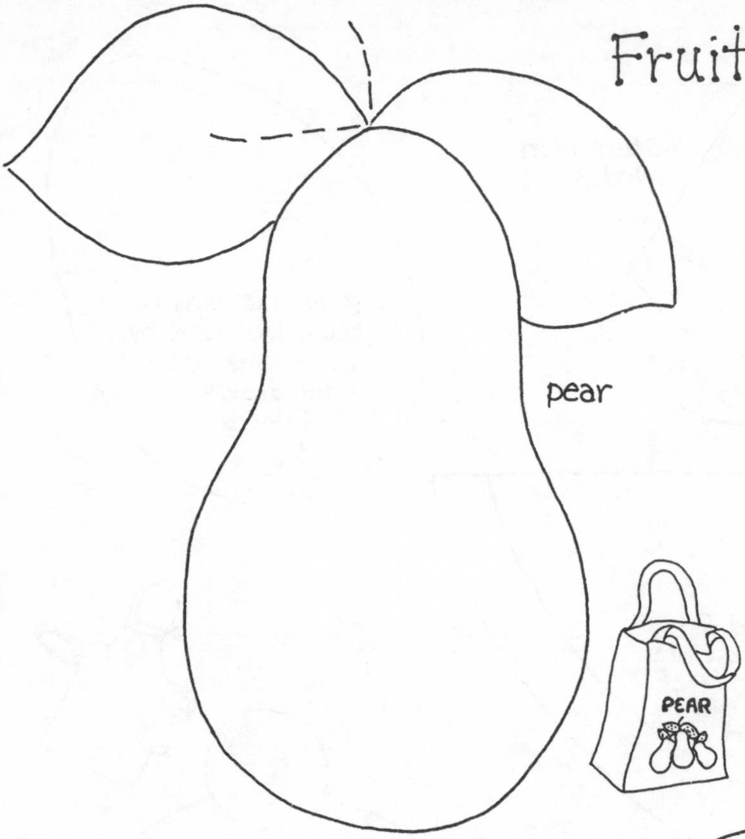

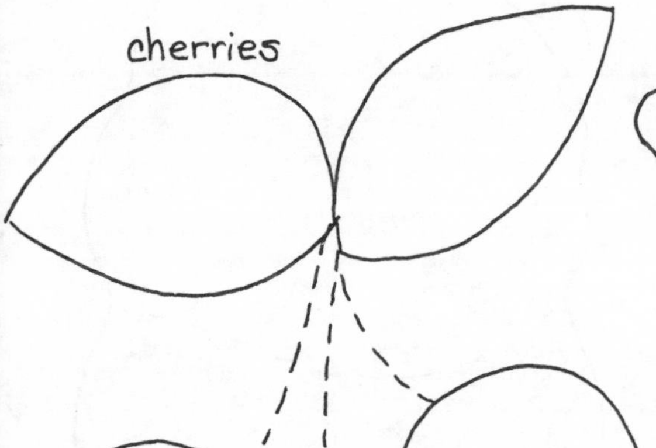

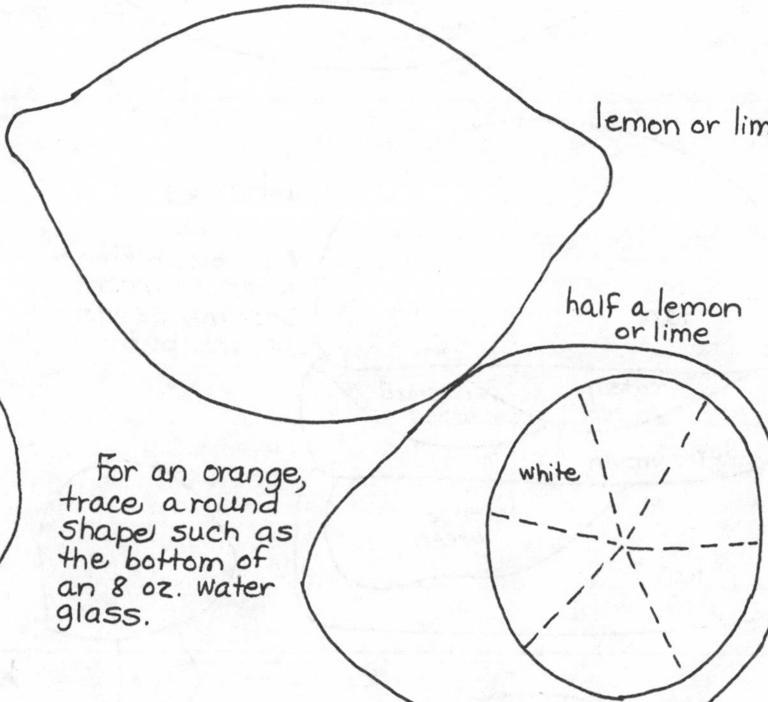

pear

grapes

PEAR

cherries

lemon or lime

half a lemon
or lime

white

For an orange,
trace a round
shape such as
the bottom of
an 8 oz. water
glass.

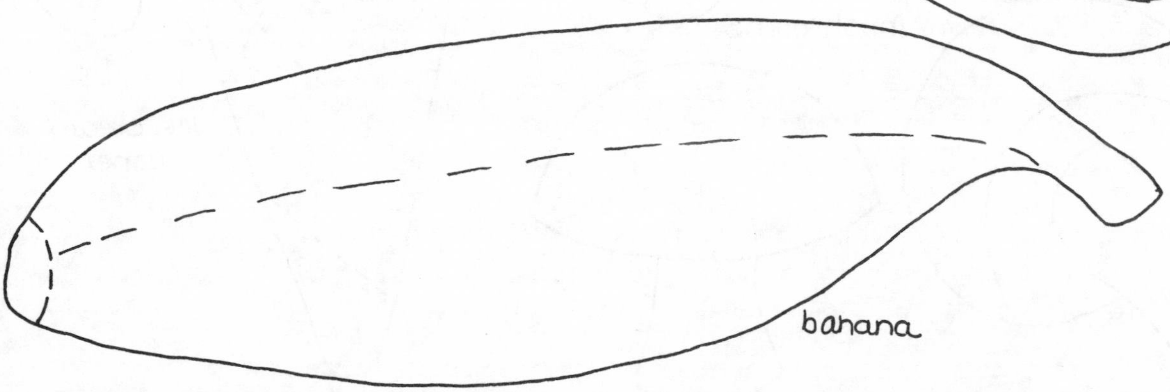

banana

Food

watermelon wedge

red

green

give this egg a "country" look by cutting it from light brown fabric

use red solid fabric or red polka dots for the center of this slice of watermelon

green

hamburger

tan

Add brown French knots to make sesame seeds on the bun.

catsup red

mustard yellow

dark brown

lettuce green

tan

mushrooms

ice cream cone

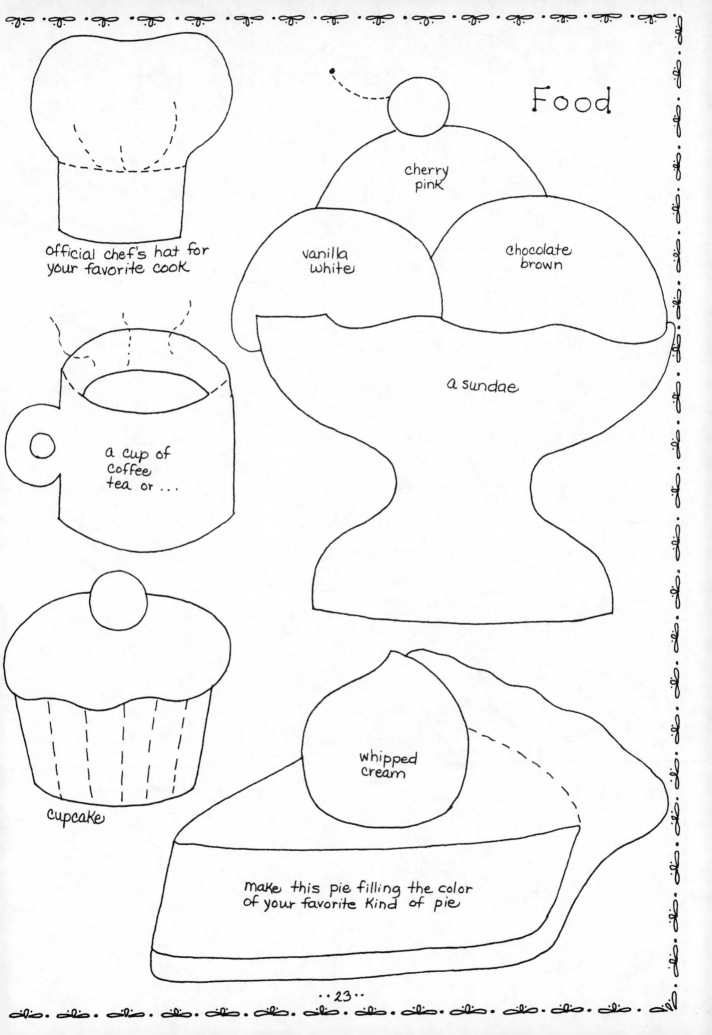

Food

official chef's hat for your favorite cook

cherry
pink

vanilla
white

chocolate
brown

a sundae

a cup of
coffee
tea or ...

whipped
cream

cupcake

make this pie filling the color
of your favorite kind of pie

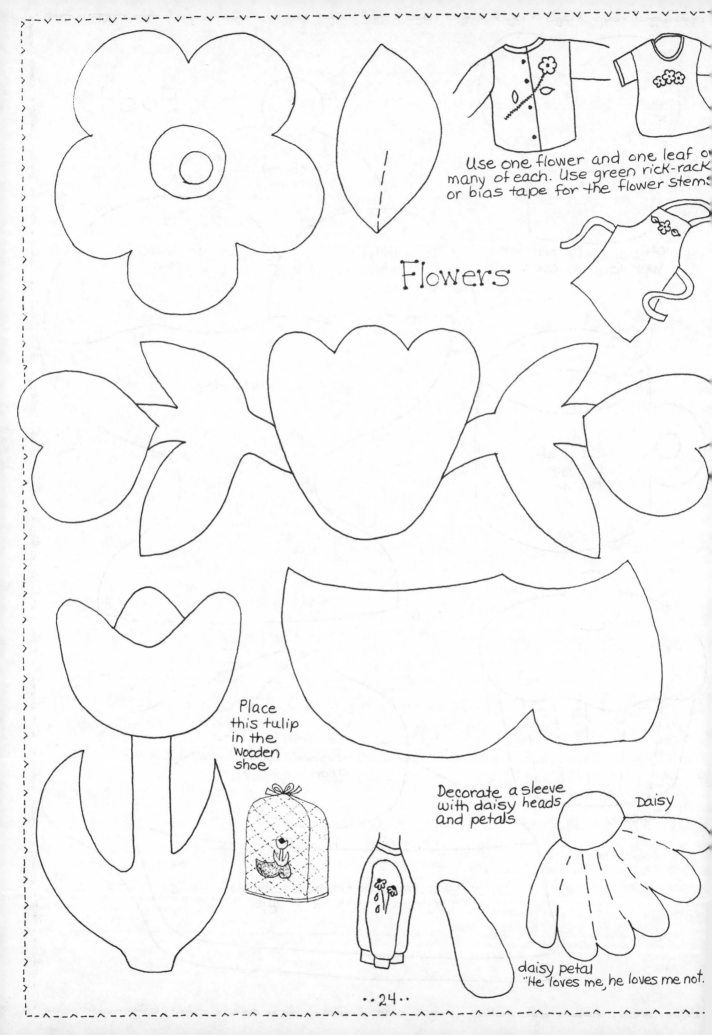

Use one flower and one leaf or many of each. Use green rick-rack or bias tape for the flower stems.

Flowers

Place this tulip in the wooden shoe

Decorate a sleeve with daisy heads and petals

Daisy

daisy petal "He loves me, he loves me not."

··24··

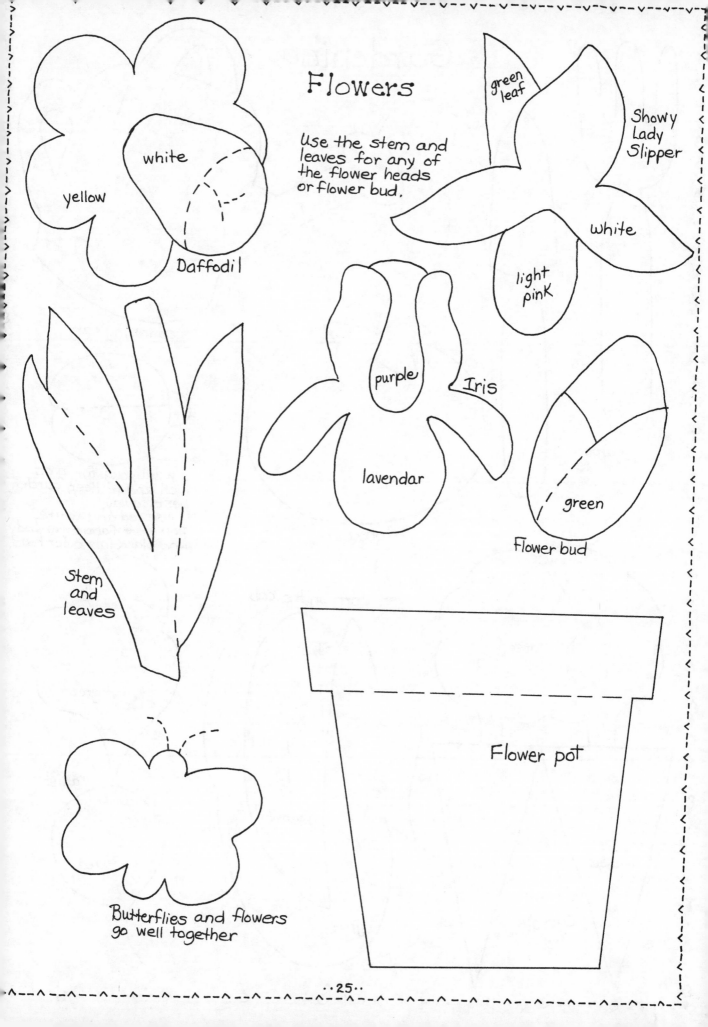

Flowers

Use the stem and leaves for any of the flower heads or flower bud.

Daffodil — yellow, white

Showy Lady Slipper — green leaf, white, light pink

Iris — purple, lavendar

Flower bud — green

Stem and leaves

Butterflies and flowers go well together

Flower pot

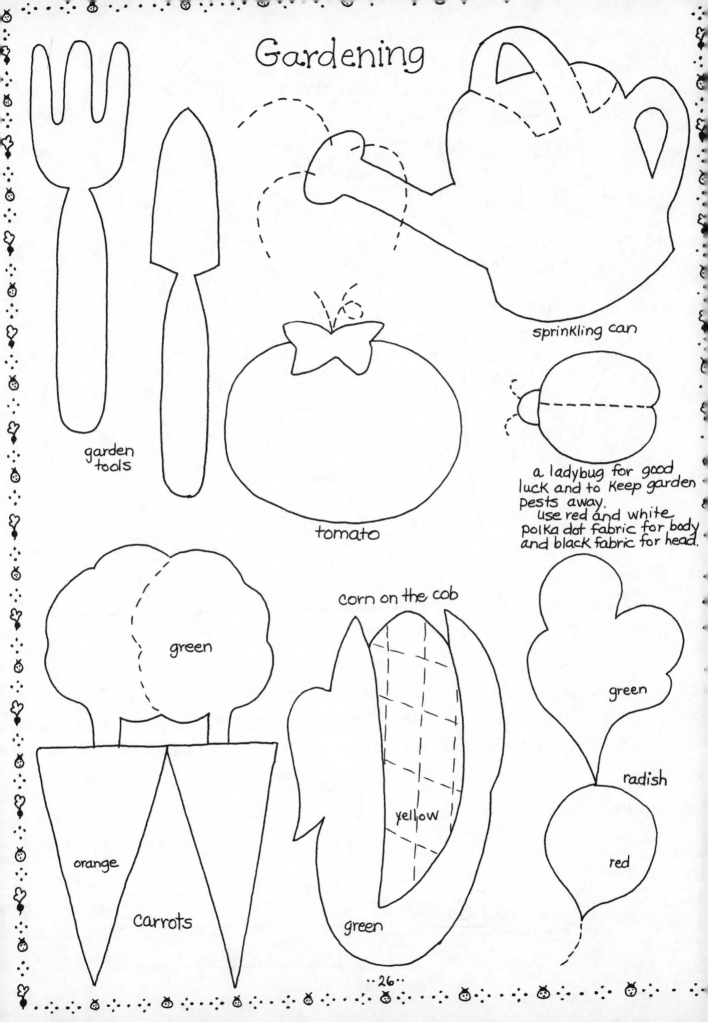

Gardening

sprinkling can

garden tools

tomato

a ladybug for good luck and to keep garden pests away.
use red and white polka dot fabric for body and black fabric for head.

corn on the cob

green

radish

green

orange

carrots

yellow

green

red

Keep in Touch...
with special people

telephone

rural mailbox

MOM

DAD

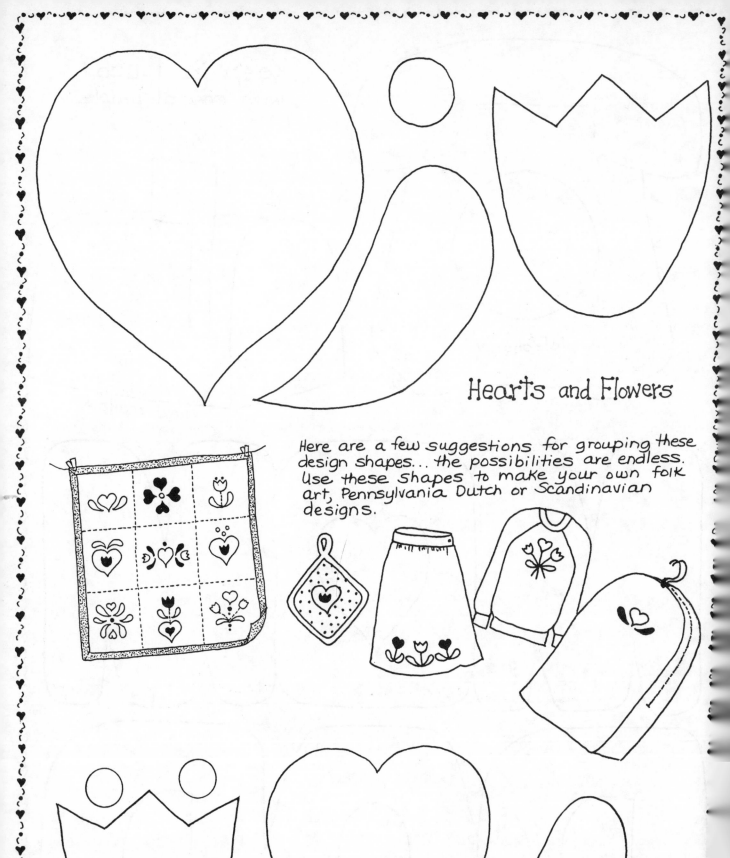

Hearts and Flowers

Here are a few suggestions for grouping these design shapes... the possibilities are endless. Use these shapes to make your own folk art, Pennsylvania Dutch or Scandinavian designs.

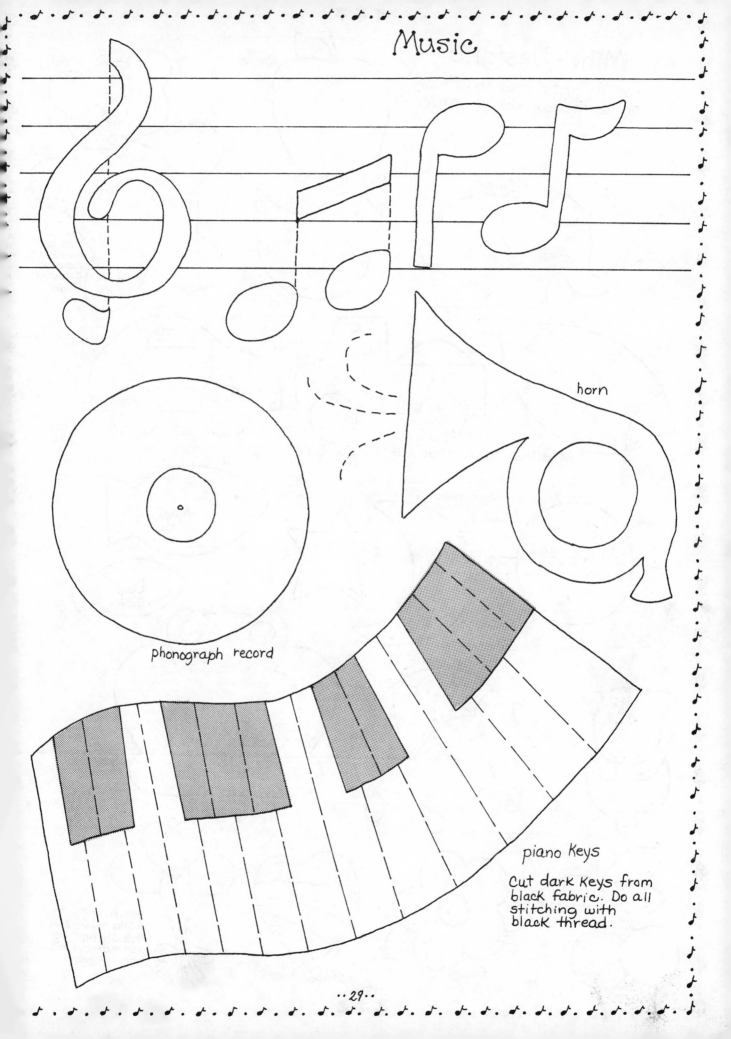

Music

horn

phonograph record

piano Keys

Cut dark keys from black fabric. Do all stitching with black thread.

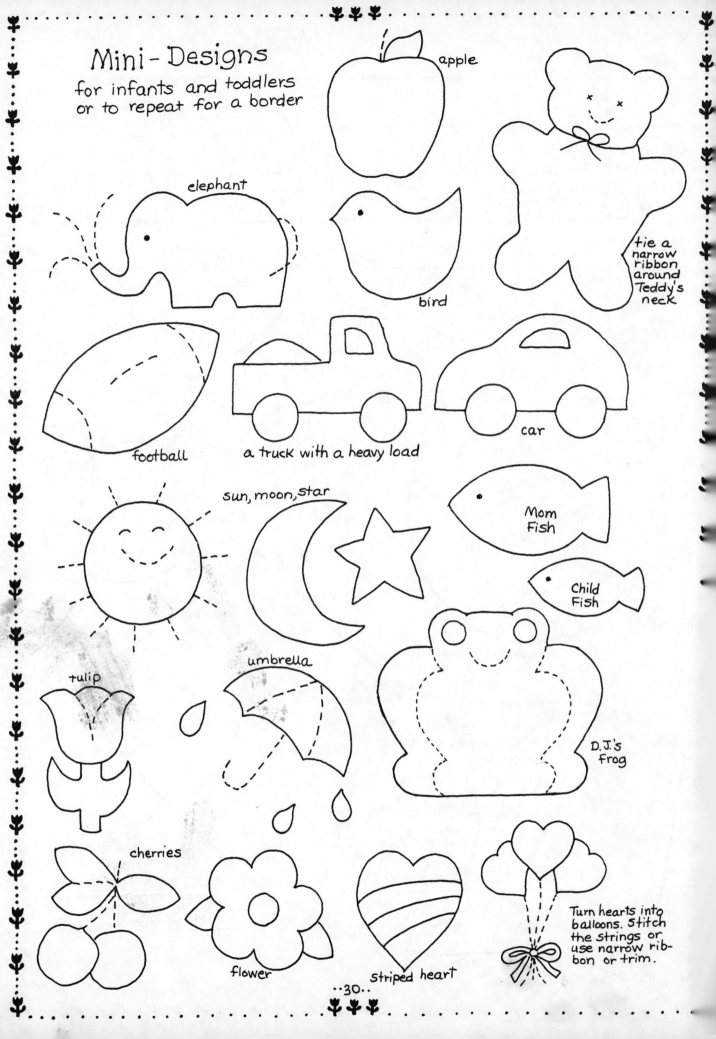

Mini-Designs
for infants and toddlers or to repeat for a border

apple

tie a narrow ribbon around Teddy's neck

elephant

bird

football

a truck with a heavy load

car

sun, moon, star

Mom Fish

Child Fish

tulip

umbrella

D.J.'s Frog

cherries

flower

striped heart

Turn hearts into balloons. Stitch the strings or use narrow ribbon or trim.

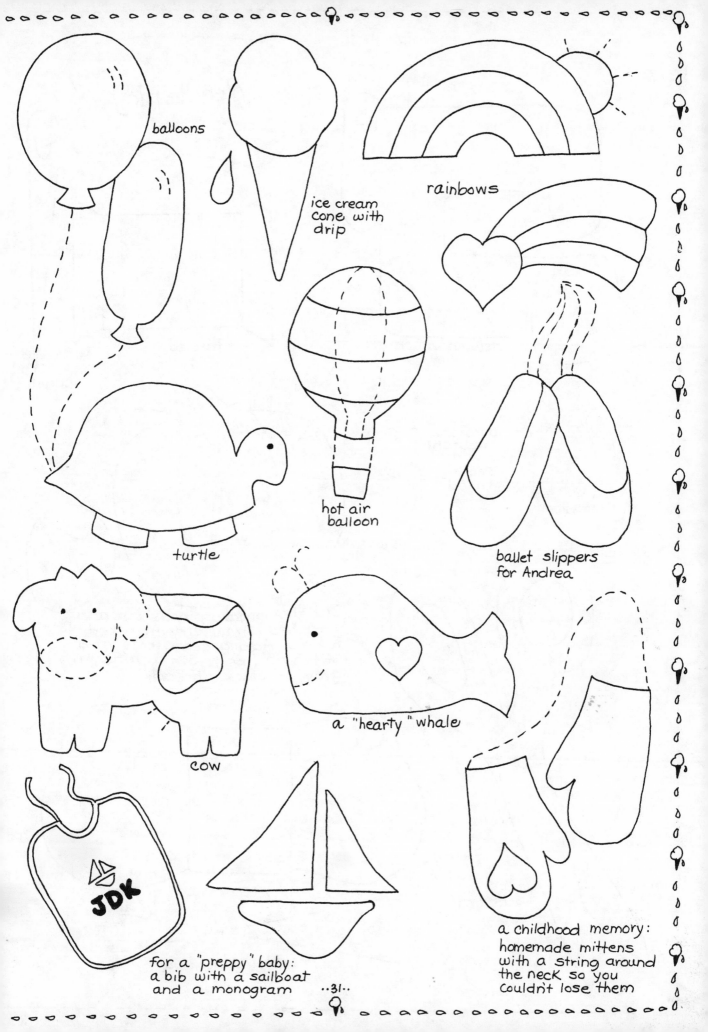

balloons

ice cream
cone with
drip

rainbows

hot air
balloon

turtle

ballet slippers
for Andrea

cow

a "hearty" whale

for a "preppy" baby:
a bib with a sailboat
and a monogram

JDK

a childhood memory:
homemade mittens
with a string around
the neck so you
couldn't lose them

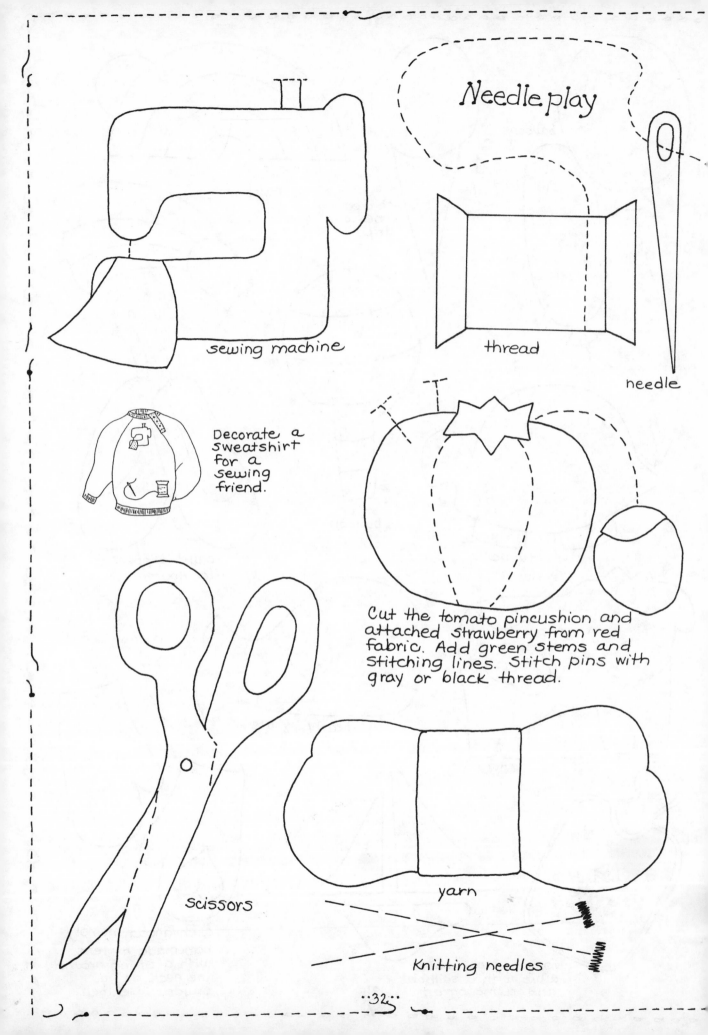

Needle play

sewing machine

thread

needle

Decorate a
sweatshirt
for a
sewing
friend.

Cut the tomato pincushion and
attached strawberry from red
fabric. Add green stems and
stitching lines. Stitch pins with
gray or black thread.

scissors

yarn

Knitting needles

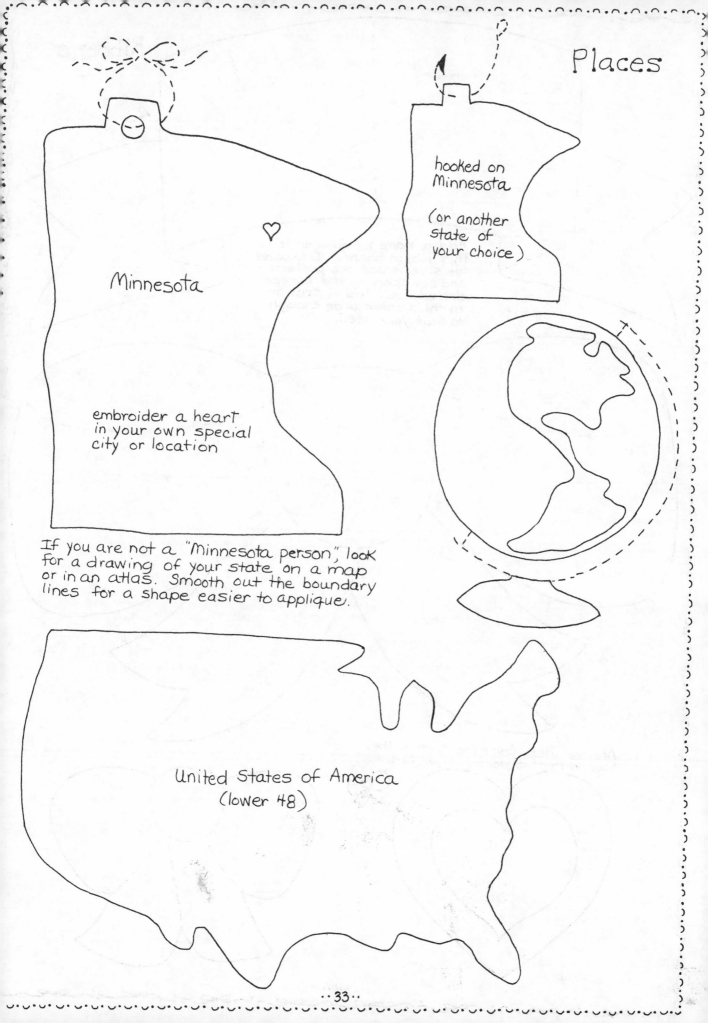

hooked on
Minnesota

(or another
state of
your choice)

Minnesota

embroider a heart
in your own special
city or location

If you are not a "Minnesota person", look
for a drawing of your state on a map
or in an atlas. Smooth out the boundary
lines for a shape easier to applique.

United States of America
(lower 48)

Add a name or number to
this ribbon banner. To expand
the size, trace the pattern
and cut open on the center
dotted line. Add a section
in the center wide enough
to suit your need.

Another idea: Cover the knot in the
bow with this double-layer heart

Rainbows

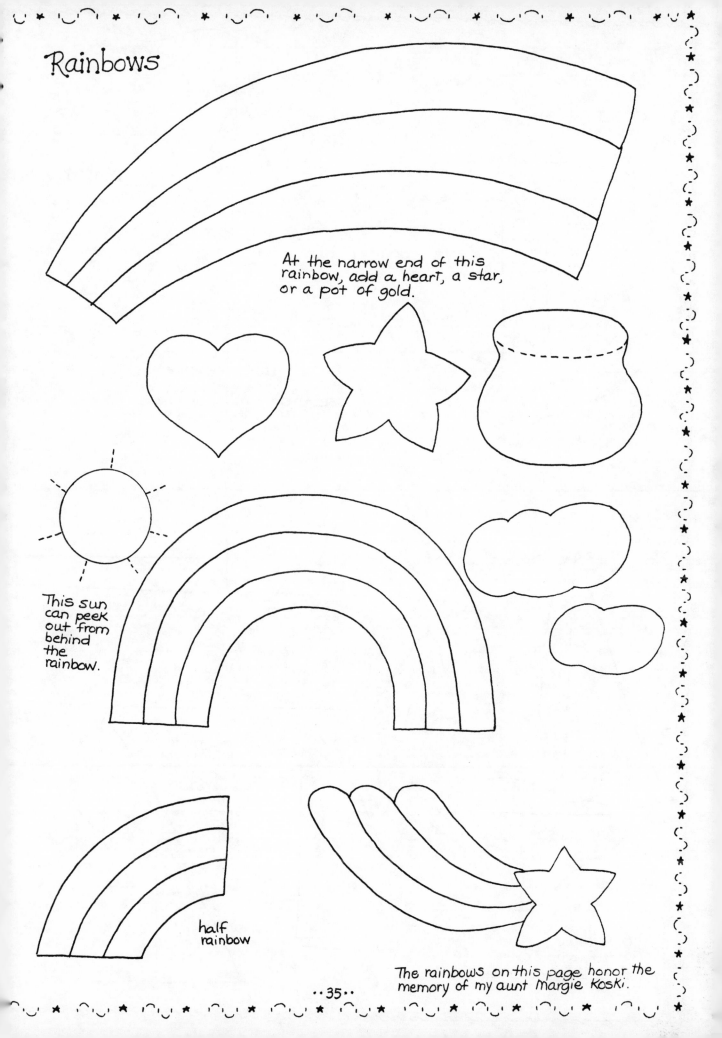

At the narrow end of this rainbow, add a heart, a star, or a pot of gold.

This sun can peek out from behind the rainbow.

half rainbow

The rainbows on this page honor the memory of my aunt Margie Koski.

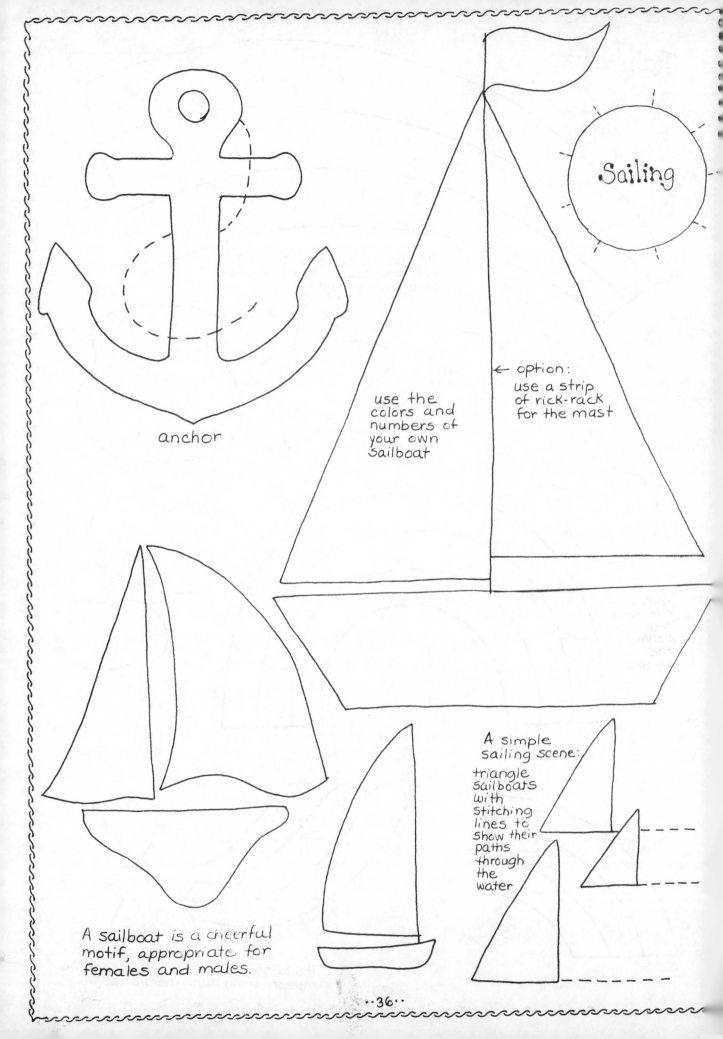

Sailing

anchor

use the colors and numbers of your own Sailboat

← option: use a strip of rick-rack for the mast

A simple sailing scene: triangle sailboats with stitching lines to show their paths through the water

A sailboat is a cheerful motif, appropriate for females and males.

Create a Scene

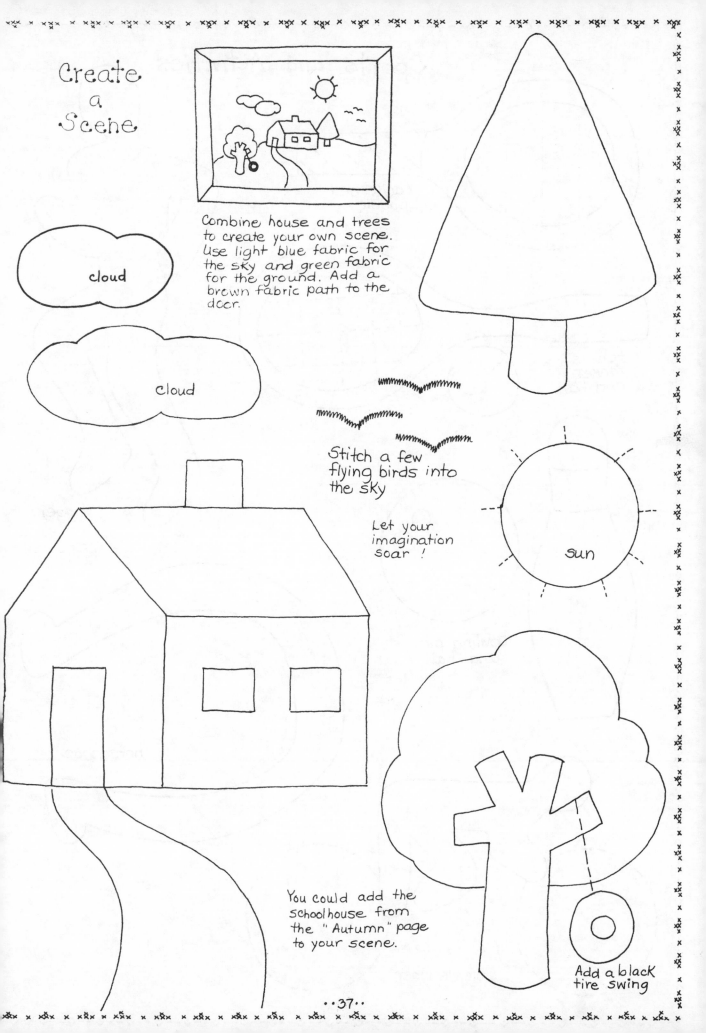

Combine house and trees to create your own scene. Use light blue fabric for the sky and green fabric for the ground. Add a brown fabric path to the door.

cloud

cloud

Stitch a few flying birds into the sky

Let your imagination soar !

sun

You could add the schoolhouse from the "Autumn" page to your scene.

Add a black tire swing

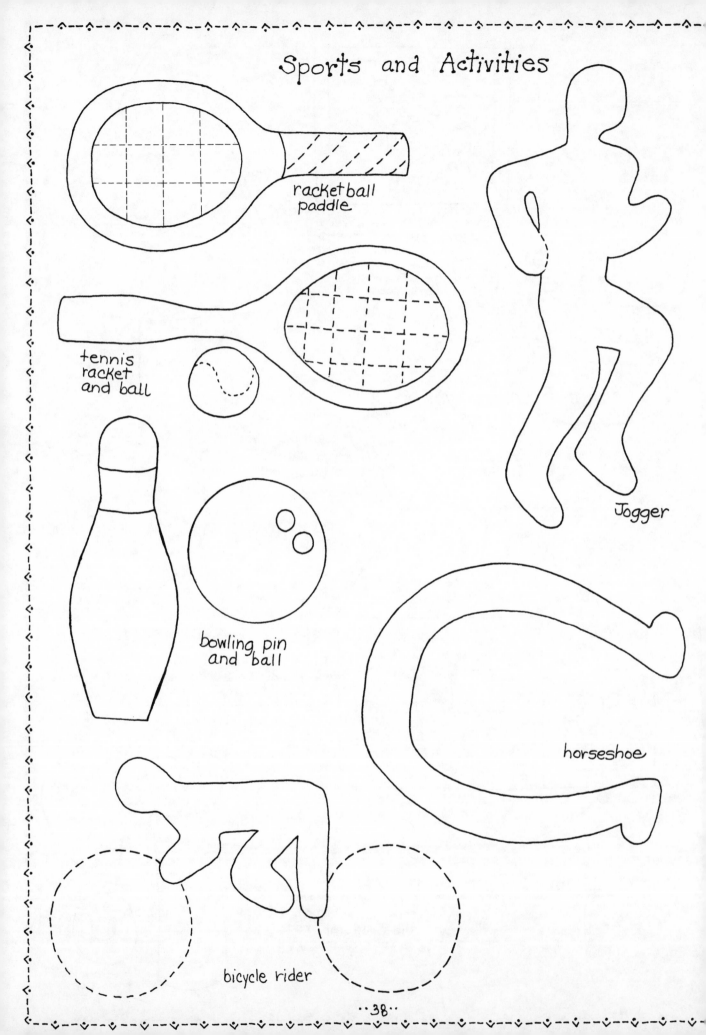

Sports and Activities

racketball paddle

tennis racket and ball

bowling pin and ball

Jogger

horseshoe

bicycle rider

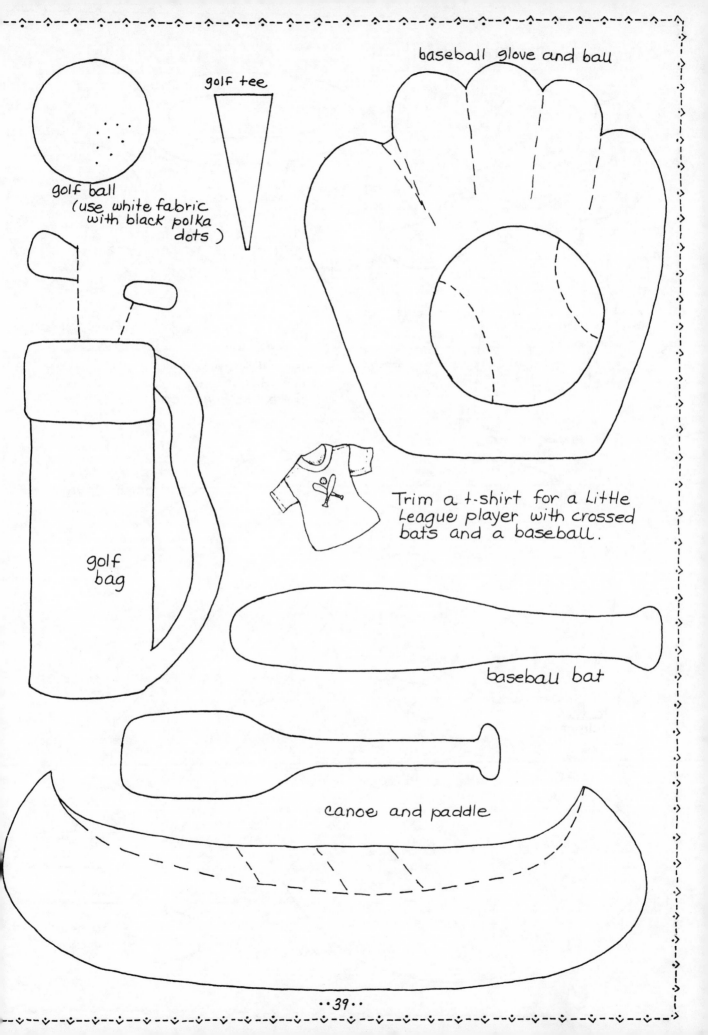

golf ball
(use white fabric
with black polka
dots)

golf tee

baseball glove and ball

golf
bag

Trim a t-shirt for a Little
League player with crossed
bats and a baseball.

baseball bat

canoe and paddle

More Sports and Activities

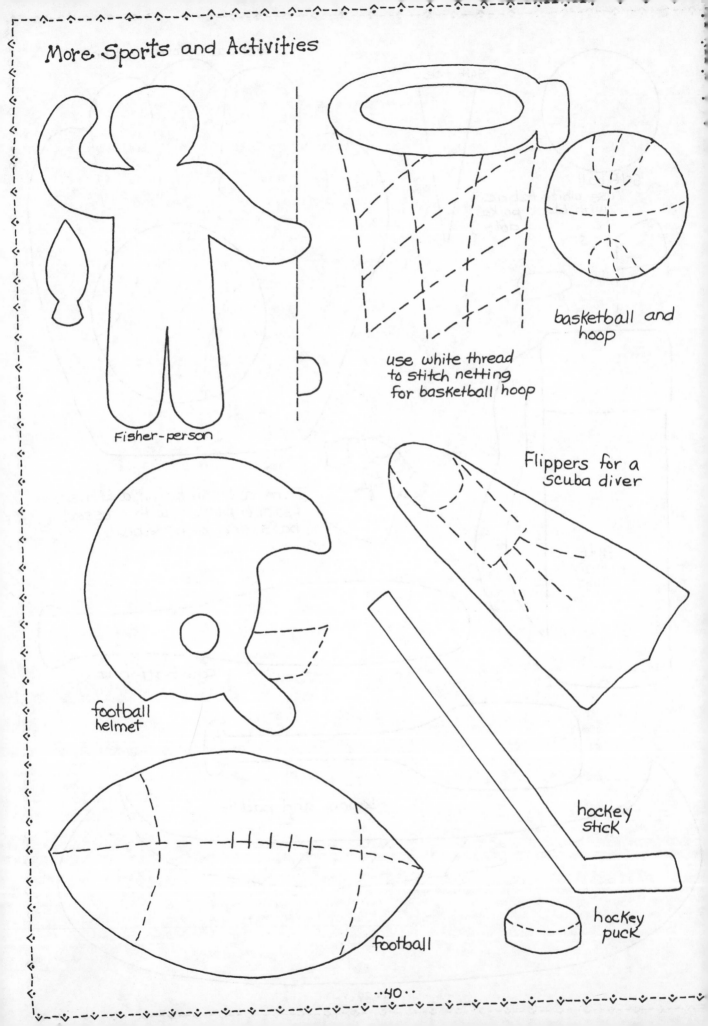

Fisher-person

basketball and hoop

use white thread
to stitch netting
for basketball hoop

Flippers for a
scuba diver

football
helmet

hockey
stick

hockey
puck

football

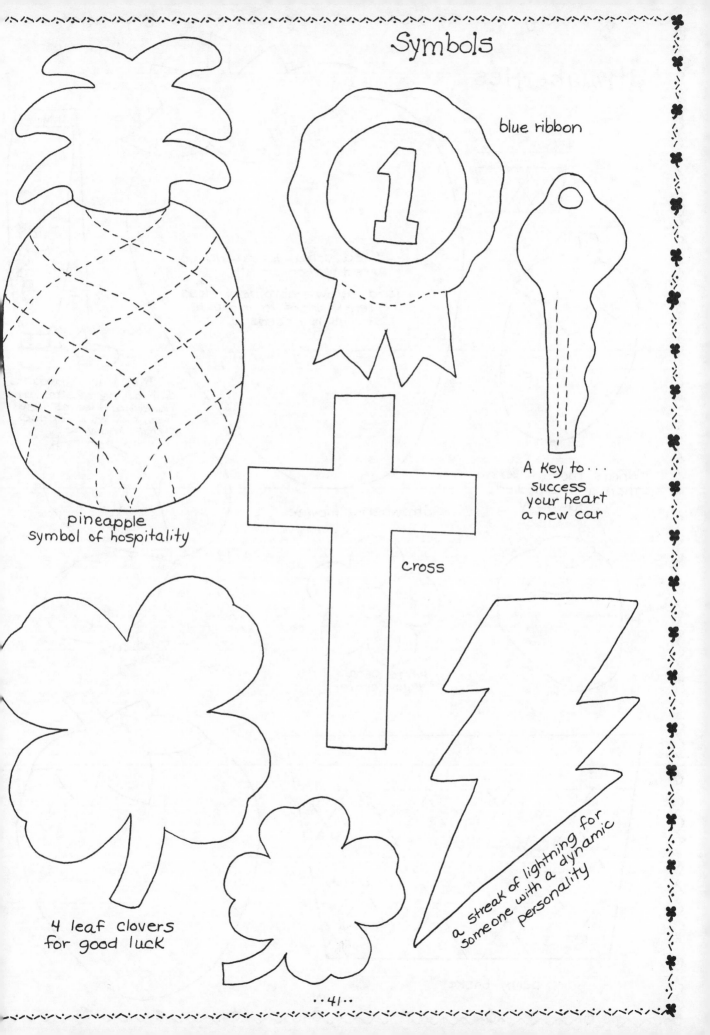

blue ribbon

pineapple
symbol of hospitality

A key to...
success
your heart
a new car

cross

4 leaf clovers
for good luck

a streak of lightning for
someone with a dynamic
personality

Strawberries

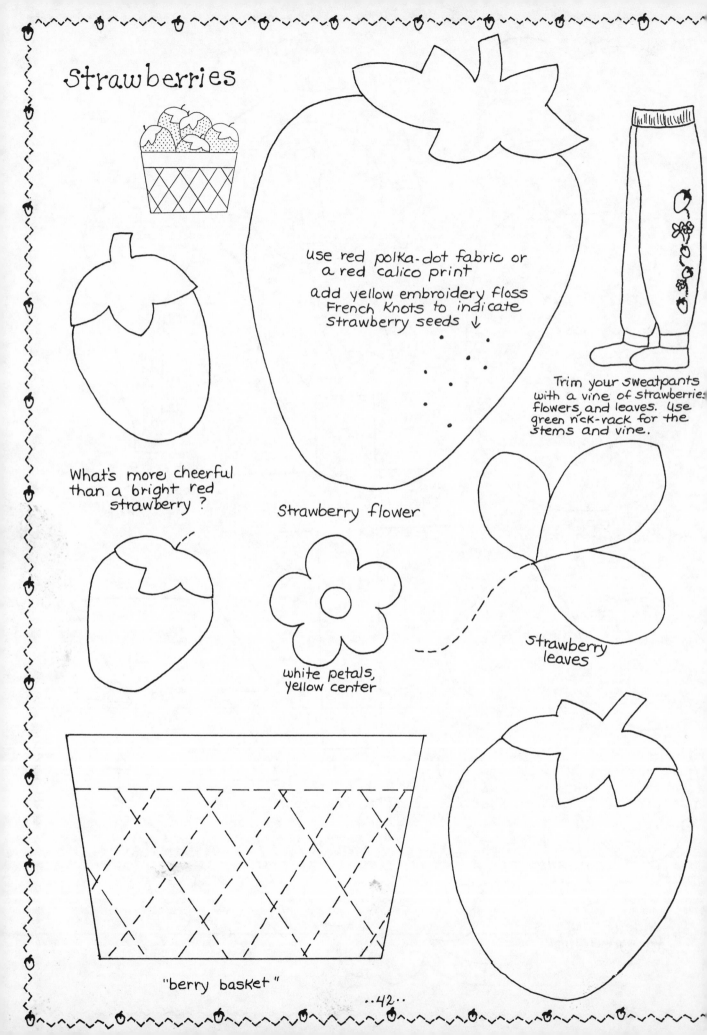

use red polka-dot fabric or a red calico print

add yellow embroidery floss French Knots to indicate strawberry seeds ↓

Trim your sweatpants with a vine of strawberries, flowers, and leaves. Use green ric-rack for the stems and vine.

What's more cheerful than a bright red strawberry?

Strawberry flower

white petals, yellow center

strawberry leaves

"berry basket"

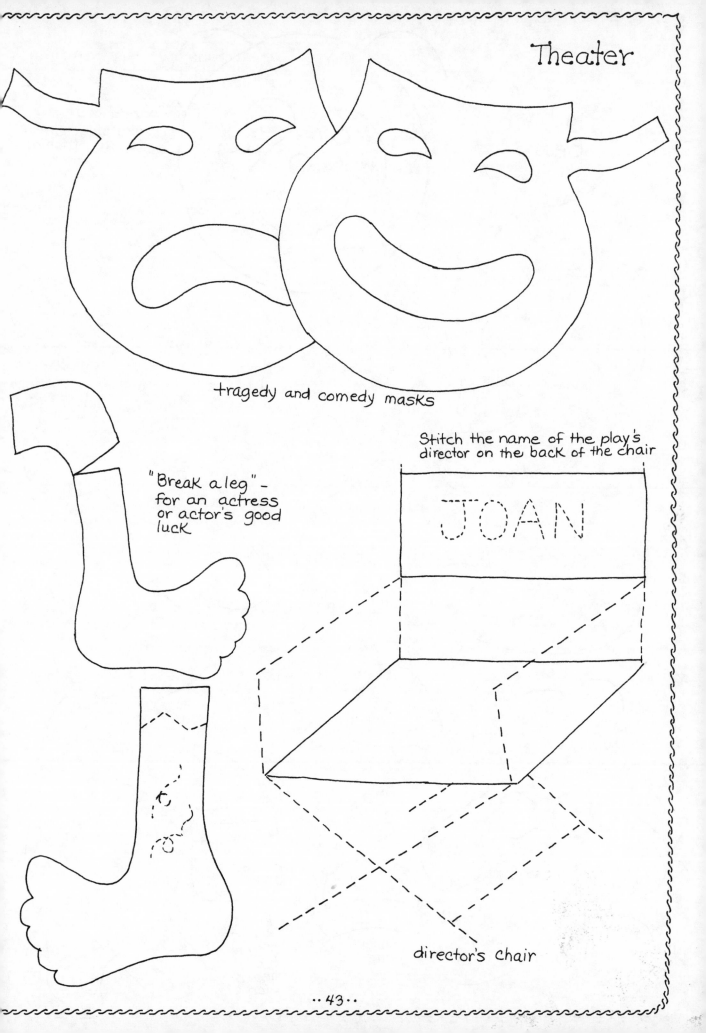

tragedy and comedy masks

"Break a leg" - for an actress or actor's good luck

Stitch the name of the play's director on the back of the chair

JOAN

director's chair

Teddy Bears

panda bear
use black thread for all stitching

black

black

black

black

white

white

cap

sailor cap

picnic basket for teddy bears' picnic

Dress the Teddy Bear

a wool scarf to wear around the neck

bowtie

t-shirt

trim on dotted lines
to make a vest.
add vest buttons

pink tutu
and ballet slippers

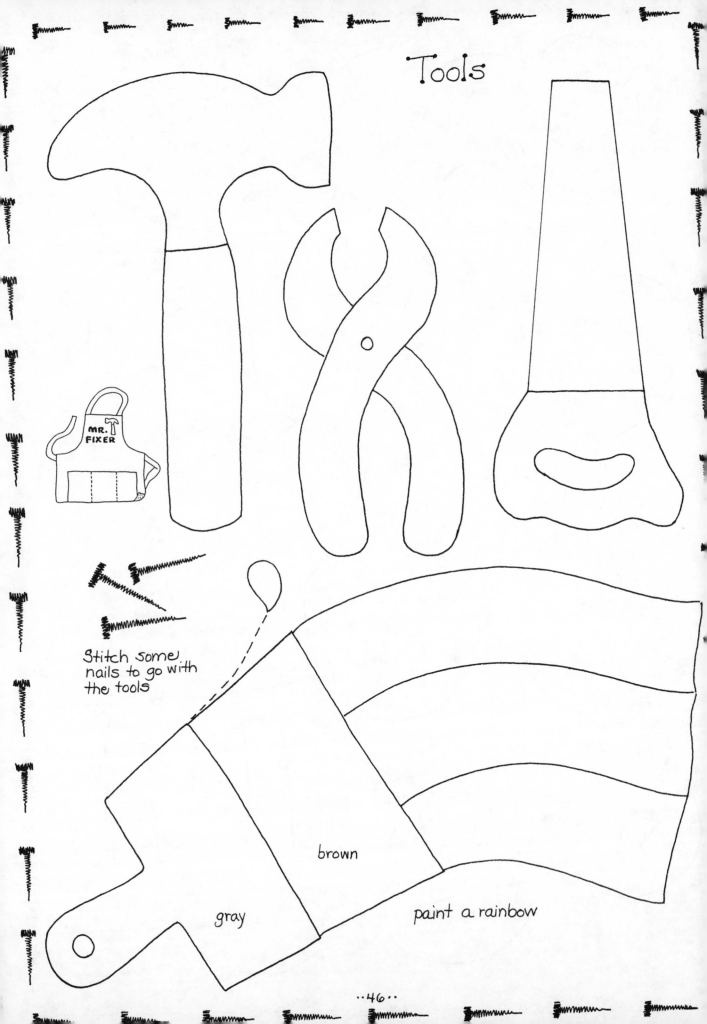

Tools

MR. FIXER

Stitch some nails to go with the tools

brown

gray

paint a rainbow

Transportation

tow truck

use fabric circles or large buttons for wheels

USA

rocket

ship - perhaps the cruise ship to the Caribbean

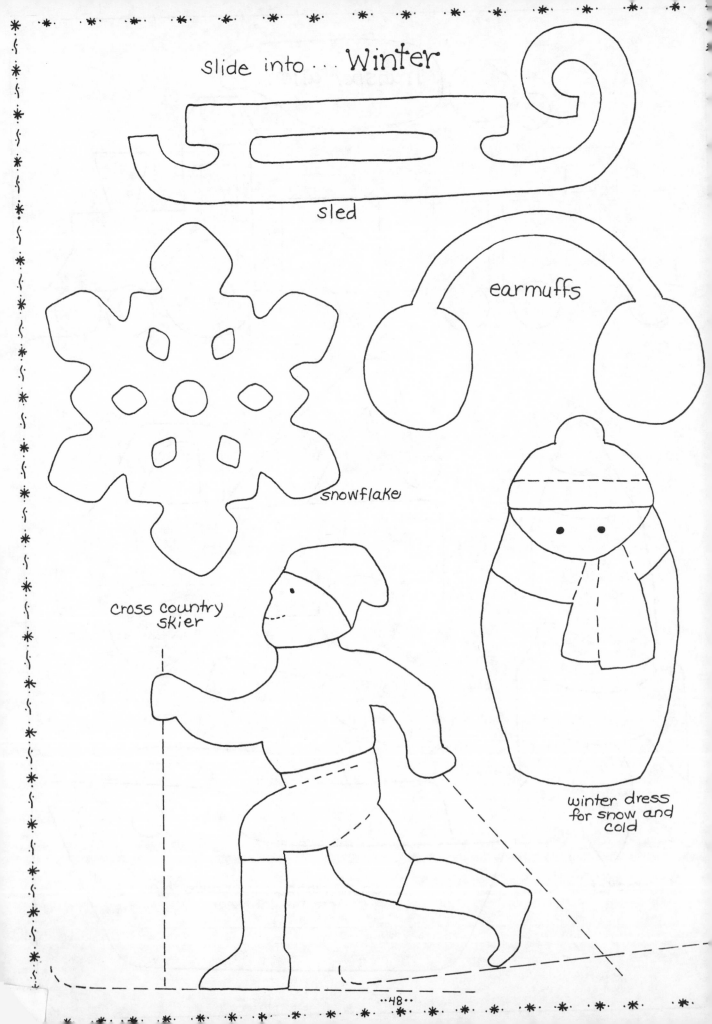

slide into... **Winter**

sled

earmuffs

snowflake

cross country skier

winter dress for snow and cold

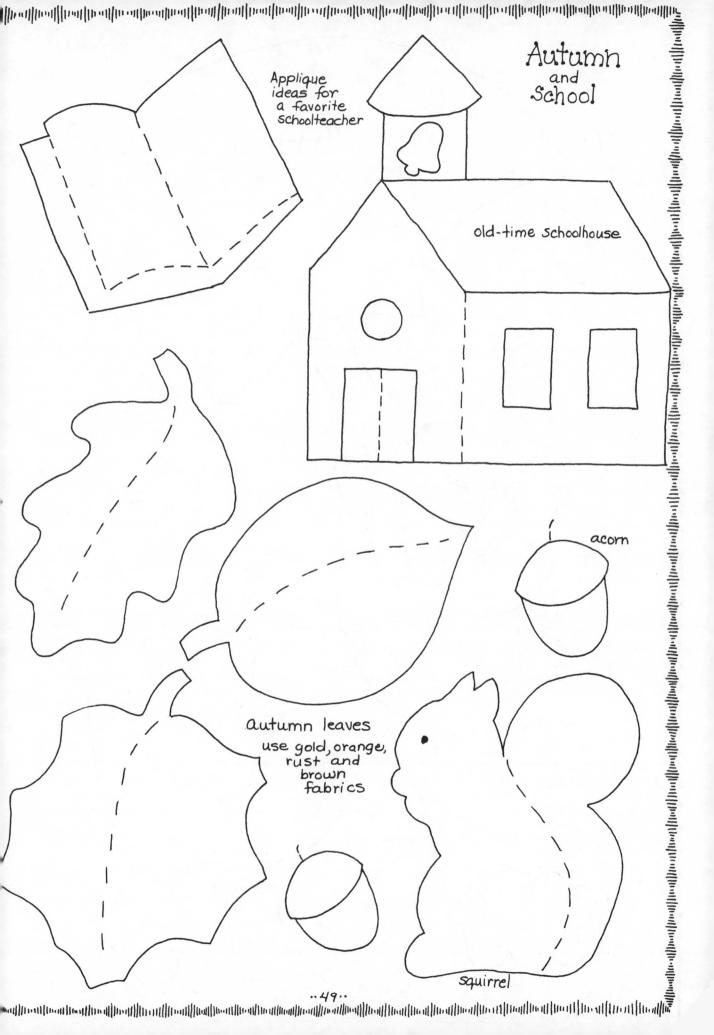

Applique ideas for a favorite schoolteacher

Autumn
and
School

old-time schoolhouse

acorn

autumn leaves

use gold, orange, rust and brown fabrics

squirrel

Spring

Stitch lines
of raindrops
with
transparent
nylon thread

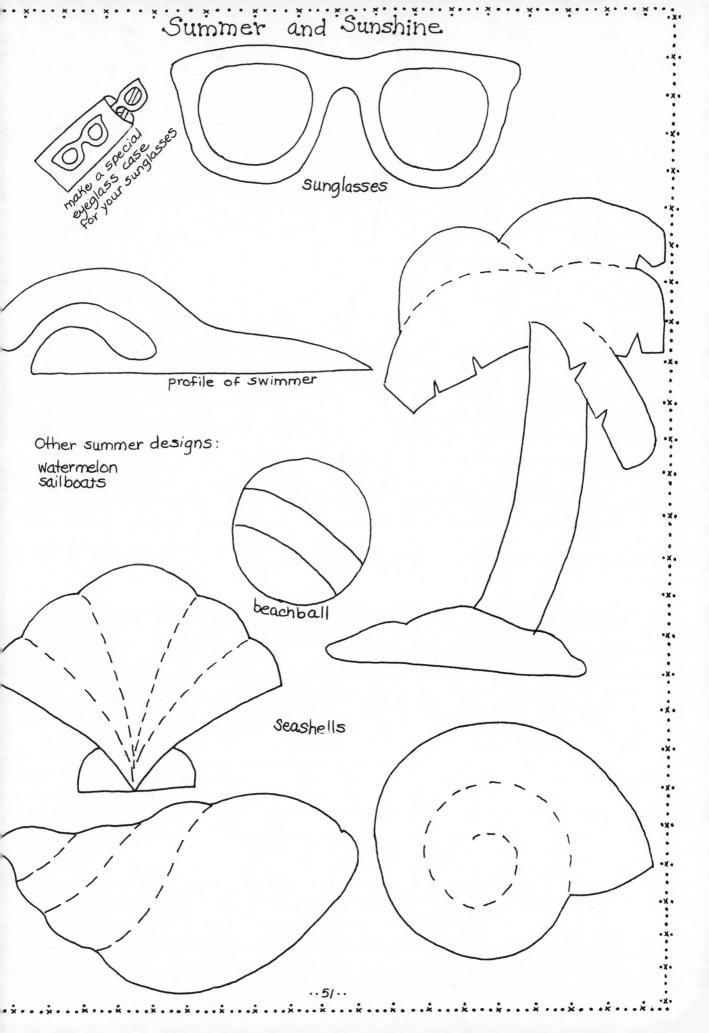

make a special eyeglass case for your sunglasses

sunglasses

profile of swimmer

Other summer designs:
watermelon
sailboats

beachball

seashells

ABCDE

FGHIJK

LMNOP

QRSTU

VWXY

Z!?& ampersand
the "and"
symbol

ABCDEFG
HIJKLM
NOPQRST
UVWXYZ

reverse 6 to get 9

ampersand - the "and" symbol

Index

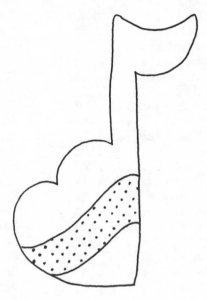

A Note from the Heart

Dear Reader,

I hope you have found many designs to stir your creativity. Though I planned this book for applique work, I know there are other uses for the designs. I would be interested to know how you are using them.

More applique designs can be found in my books *Designer Sweatshirts*
MORE Designer Sweatshirts
and in a folder of Minnesota and nature applique designs. For a free brochure, send a 22¢ stamp to

Mary's Productions
Box 87 Dept B2
Aurora, Minnesota 55705

Thanks for your interest and support!

Mary Mulari